I0824504

AROUND TOWN

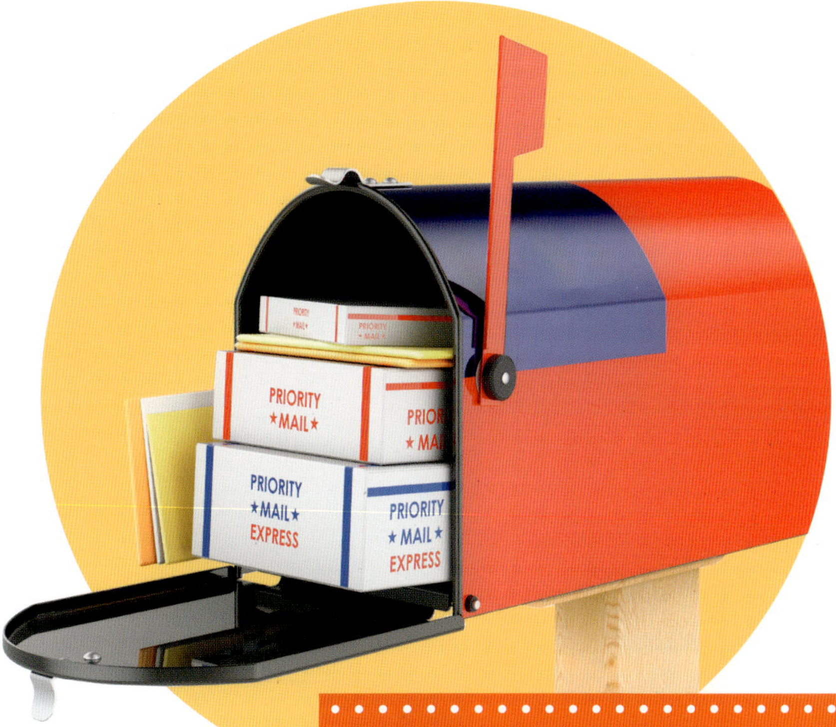

POST OFFICE

by Alissa Thielges

lobby

P.O. box

Look for these words and pictures as you read.

tray

scale

You got a letter.
Where did it come from?
The post office!

The post office moves mail.
Letters are mail.
So are packages.

lobby

Look at the lobby.
You can send a package.
You can buy stamps.

Post Office
OVERNIGHT
NOT OVERPRICED
EXIT
MAIL DROP

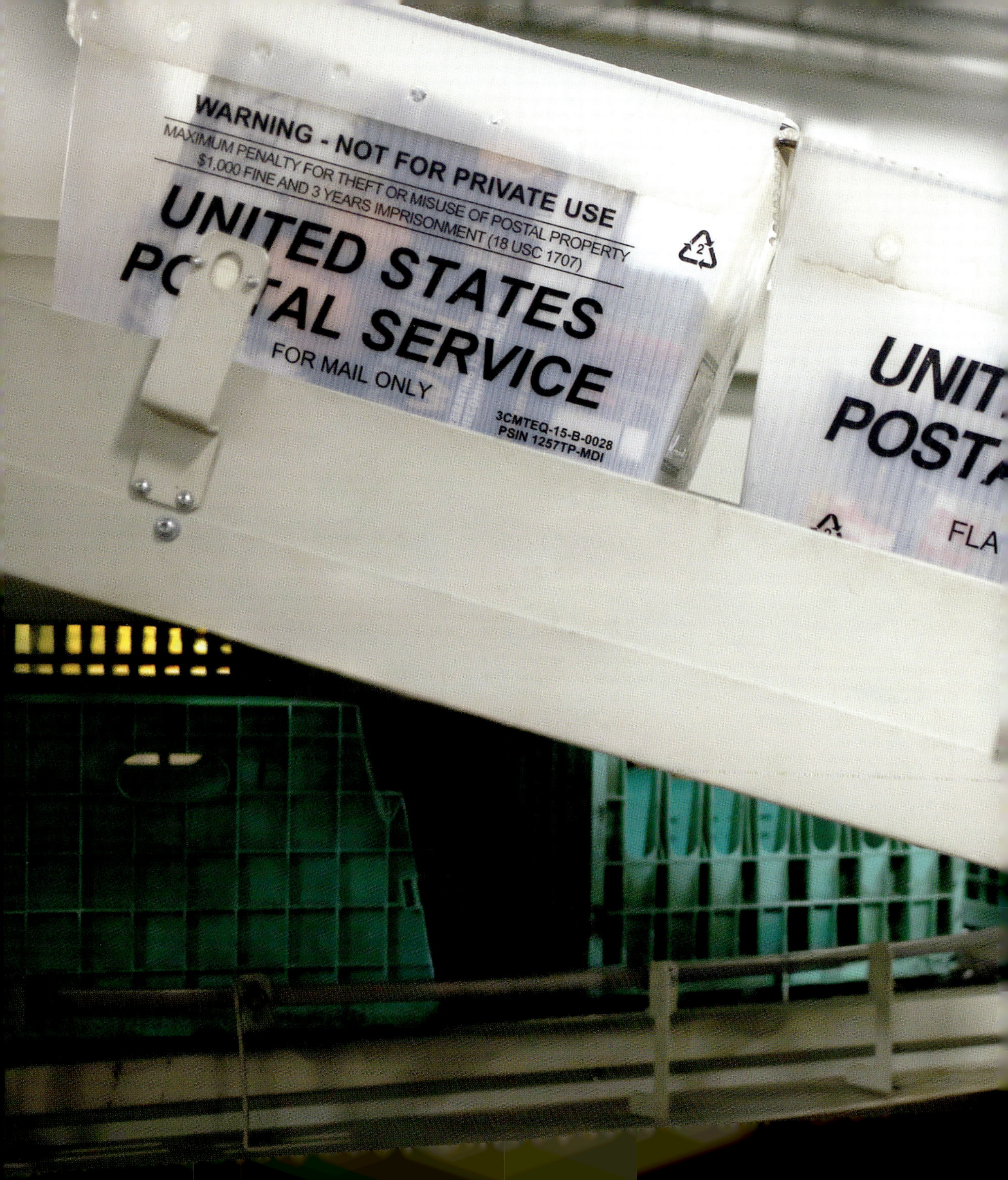
WARNING - NOT FOR PRIVATE USE
MAXIMUM PENALTY FOR THEFT OR MISUSE OF POSTAL PROPERTY
$1,000 FINE AND 3 YEARS IMPRISONMENT (18 USC 1707)
UNITED STATES
PO TAL SERVICE
FOR MAIL ONLY
3CMTEQ-15-B-0028
PSIN 1257TP-MDI

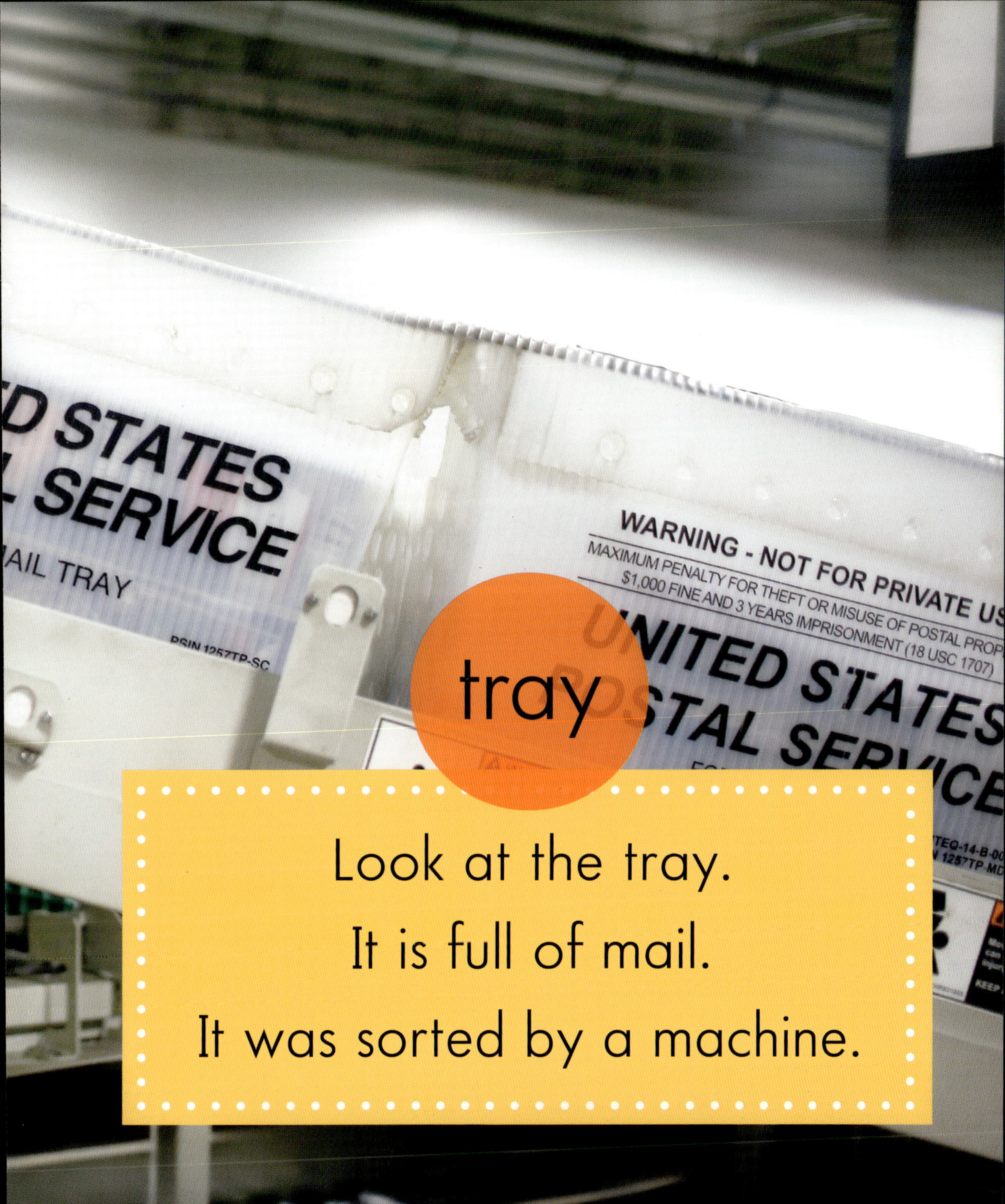

tray

Look at the tray.
It is full of mail.
It was sorted by a machine.

Look at the scale.
It weighs the mail.
Heavy mail costs more to ship.

0.0
HOLD
kg lb
Max : 50LB d=0.1OZ

P.O. box

Look at the P.O. box.
Some people do not
have a mailbox.
They pick up their mail here.

107
117
127
118
128

A mail van pulls out.
Time to deliver!

lobby

P.O. box

Did you find?

tray

scale

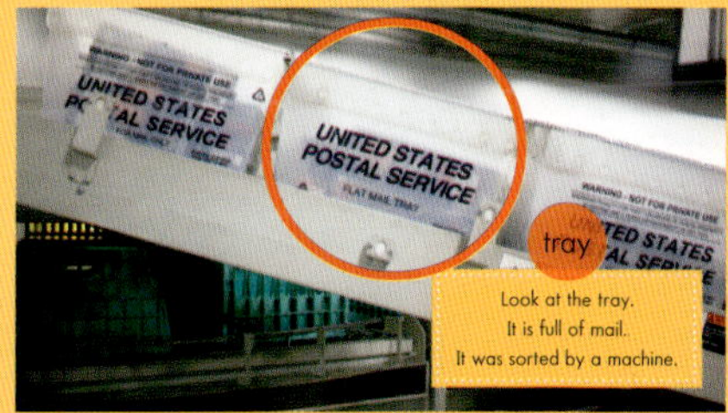

Spot is published by Amicus and Amicus Ink
P.O. Box 227, Mankato, MN 56002
www.amicuspublishing.us

Copyright © 2025 Amicus.
International copyright reserved in all countries.
No part of this book may be reproduced in any form without written permission from the publisher.

Library of Congress Cataloging-in-Publication Data
Names: Thielges, Alissa, 1995– author.
Title: Post office / by Alissa Thielges.
Other titles: Oficina de correos. English
Description: Mankato, MN : Amicus Learning, [2025] | Series: Spot around town | Audience: Ages 4–7 | Audience: Grades K-1 | Summary: "A search-and-find book about post offices reinforces new vocabulary to build reading success while close-up images of places and buildings captivate young audiences. A great early social studies book to inspire learning about communities on field trips for kindergartners and first graders"— Provided by publisher.
Identifiers: LCCN 2023045030 (print) | LCCN 2023045031 (ebook) | ISBN 9781645497370 (hardcover) | ISBN 9781645497455 (ebook)
Subjects: LCSH: Postal service—Juvenile literature.
Classification: LCC HE6078 .T4818 2025 (print) | LCC HE6078 (ebook) | DDC 383–dc23/eng/20231122
LC record available at https://lccn.loc.gov/2023045030
LC ebook record available at https://lccn.loc.gov/2023045031

Printed in China

Rebecca Glaser, editor
Deb Miner, series designer
Kim Pfeffer, book designer and photo researcher

Photos by Alamy Stock Photo/Allen Creative/Steve Allen, 3; Depositphotos/tigerfilm, 12–13; Dreamstime/Philip Openshaw, cover; Rickk6rj, 10–11; Freepik/Drazen Zigic, 4–5; machnata, 1; Getty/Luke Sharrett/Bloomberg, 8–9; Shutterstock/Sean Pavone, 6–7; Sundry Photography, 14; Unsplash/Brannon Morrissy, cover